LARRY NIX

From the Torments of Hell to
the Glories of Heaven

LARRY NIX

From the Torments of Hell to
the Glories of Heaven

WRITTEN BY
KEITH NIX

Larry Nix
From the Torments of Hell to the Glories of Heaven

by Keith Nix

Published by The Lift Publishing Group

KeithNix.org

All scripture references are taken from the King James Version (KJV).

Any italicization or words in brackets added to scripture quotations are the author's additions for emphasis or clarity.

Prepared for Publication by The Lift Publishing Group.

Special Market Sales
Organizations, churches, pastors, and small group leaders can receive special discounts when purchasing this book and other resources from Keith Nix Ministries and The Lift Church. For information, please call 865-773-0488 or visit us at TheLiftChurch.tv.

ISBN 978-0-578-93611-6 (trade paper)

CONTENTS

FOREWORD

You have in your hands an inspirational story of a child, who against all odds, experienced what it means to rise from the torments of hell to the glories of Heaven. I didn't see the torment, personally, but I witnessed, firsthand, the aftereffects of the physical, emotional, and mental abuse of a child becoming a man.

Larry and I met at the tender age of 13, fell in love at 14, got engaged at 15, and married at 16. We encountered the highs and lows of 54 years of marriage, four amazing children, six incredible grandkids, and two great grandkids. This book is his testimony, his story. His testimony, as my eldest son has said many times, is also his family's testimony.

For those of you who have experienced any form of abuse, whether by the hand of a spouse, a parent, a family member, or a stranger, don't believe the lie that you can never rise above and be more than the abuser made you believe about yourself.

Although, he did not talk about it often, I knew his past tried to haunt and hound him throughout his life. At times, he gave in to the feeling of insecurity, the fear of rejection, and the memory of pain. Most of the time, however, he rose above through prayer and surrender.

My husband wasn't highly educated, but he was anointed. He carried the surest word of prophecy of anyone I know. He walked under a unique calling and assignment. Be encouraged, the Lord can use you regardless of your ability or capability. He's just looking for your availability. *Philippians 4:13 says, "I can do all things through Christ which strengtheneth me."*

This book was not written to garner sympathy or stir feelings of pity. It was written to inspire, encourage, and help you realize your potential in Christ. As you read Larry's story, I pray it ministers to you, especially if you're experiencing or have experienced some of the same things you'll read about in this book. And remember, you're bigger than your circumstances! Your life doesn't have to be measured by your past, background, or social status. The Lord wants your life to be all He created it to be. Jesus said, *"The thief cometh not, but for to steal, and to kill, and to destroy: I am come that they might have life, and that they might have it more abundantly." John 10:10.*

My husband always said, "Do you want to know what I want on my tombstone? (And, I'm not talking about a pizza!) I want, '…I was not disobedient unto the heavenly vision.'" [Acts 26:19]

So, that's what we did! He certainly was obedient to the heavenly call. I was honored to walk beside him in ministry and marriage.

Keith Nix is not only the author of this book but our son. He spent a lot of time with his dad traveling in joint-revivals since he was a child. He served as the co-pastor of the church in Asheville for 15 years. And as the director of Camp Tribe, Keith invited his Dad as one of the keynote speakers for 22 years. In that time He heard Larry's testimony numerous times and it shows in his writing.

Larry and Ramona Nix
(In the Early Years of Marriage)

Keith's purpose in writing his dad's testimony is that it will minister hope and healing to those who read it. May you be as blessed, as I was as you read.

With love, from my heart,
Ramona Nix

INTRODUCTION

A FIGHTER IS BORN

1949 was a year for fighters. Olympic Gold Medalist and two-time World Heavy Weight Boxing Champion, George Foreman, was born in January. Rick Flair, the only wrestler inducted twice in the WWE Hall of Fame, was born in February. Then, on September twelfth, one of the greatest fighters of our generation was born. He never fought in the ring, but he went many rounds with the devil and whipped him all over the US and overseas. His name is Larry Nix, and I'm privileged to call him my dad!

The following is his story. I will attempt to tell it using his own words as much as possible. I've written from his perspective as if he is communicating directly to you. The bulk of what I share comes directly from recordings of when he shared at Camp Tribe. This book isn't a full biography; hopefully, that will come later. My goal here is to put into print what he shared with thousands of young men and women at camp.

For over twenty years, Dad lovingly labored to tell his story of rejection and redemption. Through the years, multiplied thousands of children and teens would sit enthralled at our annual youth camp as he communicated the story of his pain and joy. Thousands more tuned in from all over the world via the medium of internet streaming. Year after year, even those who had heard it multiple times would lean in to listen. They got caught up in the story, regardless of how often they heard it, crying, laughing, and soaking in the uniqueness of this man.

What many didn't know was that Dad tired of telling his story. It cost him every time he told it. He had to relive the pain each time. Even though it ends with redemption, the memory of the journey hurt every time. It also cost him the respect of some peers. They would scoff at his telling it again and again. Some questioned his reasoning and even his motives.

But he kept telling it.

Why?

Because it continued to connect with a generation of orphaned hearts from vastly varied backgrounds. On some level, they felt the rejection personally. His story was their story. As he acknowledged his pain, it permitted them to acknowledge the pain in their hearts. His story of redemption gave them the courage to believe that their tomorrows could also be victorious.

He paid the price many times over for the sake of all who responded to receive the healing life of Jesus. I hope that thousands more will know the glories of God's grace by reading the story of one of God's outstanding fighters. The enemy marked Dad for a hellish life on Earth, followed by an eternity in hell. But, before the devil even heard of Dad, God already set aside Larry Nix for the glories of Heaven. God chose him as an anointed vessel who would land many debilitating blows against the strategies of darkness.

I am privileged to have heard his story many times over and tell it many times, myself, worldwide. After all, his story is our family's story. If God hadn't redeemed him, our family wouldn't even be here. Even if, somehow Dad had met Mom, and we children were born, things would be extremely different. In all of these past years, I've never heard him tell it or told it myself when it didn't touch the hearer in a profound, life-changing way.

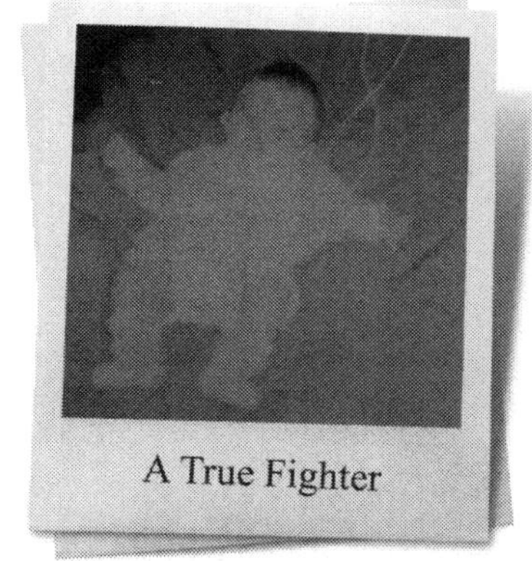
A True Fighter

My prayer is that his story will deeply touch your story and cause hope to rise in the power of God for you! I hope that putting this little volume together will cause great things for you, in you, and through you. Get ready to laugh, cry, and be touched by the goodness of God's grace and the awesomeness of His faithfulness! Now go with me and let's listen to Dad as he shares his testimony, From the Torments of Hell to the Glories of Heaven!

CHAPTER ONE

THE CRAZY WOMAN'S GOT ME!

I never knew my biological dad, Robert Nix. They tell me he was a handsome man, and I can believe it because my wife tells me I'm handsome, too (I had to get it from someone)! My dad was a wanderer. When I was just three months old, while on leave from the Army, he threatened to smash my brains against the cement block wall. I don't know why he felt that way toward me. Perhaps he was under the influence of alcohol or angered at my mom over something. I don't know, but something fueled the demons that controlled him. He walked out of our world for good before I was old enough to have any memories of him. I never saw him again.

Even though I was abandoned by my dad, the first five to six years of my life are pleasant in my memories. My grandfather's presence helped fill in the void of Dad's absence. Looking back, life wasn't that bad. It seems we primarily lived with my grandparents during that season, and they filled my days with the normal stuff little boys enjoy.

One memory that stands out is the day our crazy aunt visited. I use the word crazy because that is what my mom and others in the family called her. I remember Mom warning my sisters, Evelyn and Linda, and me about her visit. She told us that Aunt Allie had gone crazy after the death of her husband, Bob.

Bob Self was a prominent preacher of his day in the mountains of Western North Carolina. They reported that in twenty years of ministry, he won over twenty thousand to Christ in Western North Carolina and pioneered dozens of churches. He and Aunt Allie were part of the Free Will Baptist movement and were instrumental in a powerful move of God that swept the area. His ministry not only included salvation but remarkable answers to prayer, as well. I'm not sure if I was just a small child or maybe not yet born when one such miracle took place.

I remember hearing about the Lord healing the family cow. Yes. The cow. It seems the cow had gone dry and couldn't produce milk. This doesn't seem like a big deal to most now, but to a low-income family in a rural area back in the day, it was devastating. The children depended on the milk from the cow for their primary sustenance. With no money or means of bartering for a replacement, the family was in dire straits. When word reached Uncle Bob, he came, with his Bible and anointing oil in hand, going out into the small pasture. He spent a few moments with the cow, reading the Bible, pouring oil on the cow's head, and finally laid his hands on it and prayed. He walked back to the family and said, "All is well." The next day the cow produced milk and never went dry again. Glory to God!

This wasn't the only time my family experienced the healing power of prayer. When I was a small infant, I developed a severe case of thrush in my mouth which kept me from being able to feed. According to my aunts, I was dying. My grandmother sent someone in the family down to Woodfin Church of God and asked Pastor Dotson and the visiting evangelist to come and pray for me. After the revival service, they arrived late at the house and prayed for me. After prayer, the ministers instructed Mama to feed me, but I still couldn't eat. Those men of God looked at one another and concluded they hadn't prayed through. So they both went to their knees and prayed again. Getting up after a few moments, Pastor Dotson nodded to Mama and she offered me the bottle again. This time, I drank all of it. The Lord healed me in response to their prayer of faith!

People often asked Uncle Bob about what was happening with the Pentecostals, especially regarding speaking in tongues. He responded, "I've read it in the Bible, but I don't understand it. I haven't experienced it but let's not fight against it lest we be fighting against God. We may not understand it, but if it's for us, we'll receive it." He died having never experienced it, but after his death, Aunt Allie got it! She attended an old-fashioned Holy Ghost, Church of God camp meeting and received the baptism of the Holy Ghost. What he never understood or experienced, his wife experienced.

She spoke in tongues, quaked, danced under the influence, prayed, and prophesied. The family thought she had gone crazy. But she had only gone deeper into the things of God.

Well, when I was six years old, the crazy lady came to visit. Mom said, "She pitches fits everywhere she goes. She'll just start shaking and grab people and they'll fall down." Mama assured us she wouldn't let anything happen to us. She promised to keep Aunt Allie away from us. She failed! We were all outside when the car pulled up. When they opened the back door, this little old lady got out. Guess what? It hit her! She got out and started quaking, shaking, dancing, and speaking in tongues.

Larry Nix and His Grandfather

My sisters got away almost as soon as Aunt Allie arrived. She scolded them for being scantily dressed, and they took off. I didn't know they could move so fast! I stood there thinking, "Wow. They are really moving." Then I turned to run after them, but she grabbed me. I remember my heart pounding so loud I could hear it in my ears. I looked up at Mom with a pleading look, trying to communicate, "Mama, the crazy woman's got me. Help me, Mama! Don't let her hurt me!"

Holding me by my shirt collar with one hand, she somehow got a small bottle filled with olive oil out of her purse. At the moment, I didn't know what was in that bottle, and she didn't give anybody time to ask. She opened it and poured its contents all over my head. It was thick, and it ran down onto my face and down my shirt. Then she went into another one of her spells. She spoke a language I didn't recognize and shook back and forth with a few words of English peppered in like, "Hallelujah," "Praise the Lord," and "Thank you, Jesus." I shook, too, as I stood there! I wanted to run, but she had a firm grip on my shoulder and on my mind. Elvis Presley could always out-sing me and out-play me on the guitar, but that day I certainly out shook him. As terrified as I was, it also felt good and strangely peaceful. By now, I didn't think she was really going to hurt me, and my curiosity got the best of me. I wanted to see what she was going to do next.

Her next?

Her next was to prophesy! I didn't know what it was then, but God has brought it back to my mind many times through the years. As I stood there trembling, now more under the power of the Holy Spirit than fear, I had no clue regarding the changes coming to my life, and the hell I would endure over the next four years. I mean, I would truly go through hell on earth. Things happened to me I'll never be able to fully tell anyone, certainly not young men and women.

In a moment, she started speaking English again, "God has anointed this young lad and will use him greatly. His Uncle Bob's mantle is upon him. But he will walk in it with the power to heal the sick, raise the dead, cast out devils, and speak in tongues. He will be on fire with the Holy Ghost."

She turned to my mother, "Be careful how you treat him, for this one is chosen and anointed of God."

I've often wondered how different things would have been if Mom had heeded Aunt Allie's warning that day. Instead of giving heed, she just silently scoffed. When Aunt Allie left, Mom said, "She didn't hurt you, did she, son? Come here and let me wash that stuff off. I'm sorry, but she was in that fit, and I was afraid to touch her."

I had no way of knowing the significance of that "crazy woman's" obedience to the Lord on that day. I doubt she knew it either, but her prayer and words were timely. She prophetically declared over my life the calling of the Lord and watered the seed of my destiny. The Lord had her declare my future just before the enemy came into my life to turn me in a completely different direction. She prayed for Holy Ghost protection over my life just before I would need it the most. I'm convinced that little Aunt Allie's obedience is key to all the Lord has done in me, for me, and through me. Everyone God has touched through my life, including you, owes a debt of thanks to this little lady.

Prayer changes things. Prophetic prayer releases Heaven into the earth and dismantles the strategies of destruction. God sent someone that many considered just a crazy old woman to build a hedge of protection around my life for the dark years ahead of me. She most likely never knew of her important role in my story, but God used her as a key to my future and the many futures He graced my life to impact. What a joy it must have been to her when she got to Heaven and discovered the significance of just that one act of obedience!

I want to encourage you, don't underestimate the power of anointed prayer!

CHAPTER TWO

HELL ON EARTH

The details of how they met were beyond my six-year-old mind, but I remember hating the day with everything in me. He was big and physically strong. He was an evil man. Later, I came to realize that he was also a hurting man. Hurting people hurt people. My new stepdad must have lived in constant torment. His goal was to inflict pain on as many as he could, especially those closest to him.

Our tough, but otherwise, alright, lives quickly became hell on earth! We all became targets of his demonic attacks. He would often beat my mom in a drunken rage, but he unleashed his most vicious attacks on my sister and me. He especially seemed fixated on me.

I now know that demons tormented and drove him. If anyone was ever demon-possessed, and I've seen a lot during my years of ministry, indeed he was. He obviously was a functioning alcoholic on some level because he sometimes kept a job, but at home, he seemed drunk all the time. I can only describe him as wild. He wanted to hurt everything that was around him; to master and break them. He lived to take whatever and whomever and use it and them for his satisfaction. He had killed men. In fact, he was fresh out of prison, where he served time for killing a man, when Mom married him. Some of the toughest men in the city feared him. He was so wild and full of darkness.

It became a vicious cycle of living from one drunken night to another. My stepdad would get drunk and beat us, often knocking us against the wall and daring us to get up. When we tried, he would stomp us back into submission. I mean, we went through beatings. I'm not talking about corrective disciplines, but beatings. It was a torment. Our world consisted of alcohol, cussing, and evil. Everything we knew was evil, evil to the very core. He hated God. He didn't even want God mentioned unless blasphemed by cursing.

The most predictable thing about our lives was misery. I remember having to move constantly. It seemed we lived on the run. I remember being in eight schools in one year because we had to keep on the move. He was involved in illegal activity, which meant he had to stay away from the eyes of the police. And when he ran, they dragged us along. We went from misery to misery.

When I speak about being beaten, I doubt you can comprehend the horror of it. I hope you can't. I told you that while he beat us all, he seemed fixated on me. Of course, I would cuss him - repeating what I heard him say. And when I did, he would beat me more. Often when he threw us against the wall, daring us to defy him by standing, I would stand. He tried to break me. He tried to break my will completely.

I remember one night when they (my mom helped him) stripped me. As I stood naked, I trembled despite myself. I cursed them while they plaited hickory sticks together and beat me with them. The sound in the room was like the cracking of a bullwhip. It felt like what a bullwhip must feel like. Wow. How it hurt. My skin was cut, and my blood flowed. Sometimes the blood flowed until it puddled on the floor around my feet, and I passed out.

I vividly remember this night because he beat me until I passed out. When I revived, neither he nor my mom looked at me with love or pity. Instead, they glared at me in anger.

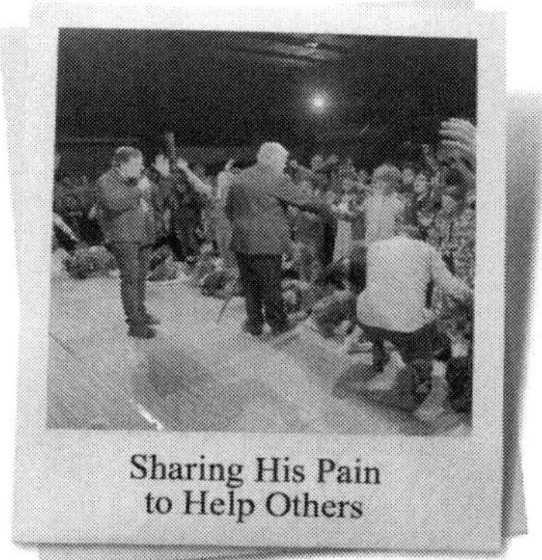

Sharing His Pain to Help Others

He cursed. "You will cry!"

"No! You can kill me, but I will not cry."

This caused him to hit me again and again until I passed out once more. When I woke up this time and still refused to cry, he started beating me again.

Finally, Mama stopped him. "We can't whip him again. If we do, we'll kill him and they'll get us for his murder."

The beatings were so severe that when Ramona and I got married, the first time she saw my back, she asked, “What in the world happened to you?”

The scars that crisscrossed my back were so many and so deep that she thought I had fallen into a barbed wire fence or something as a kid. I told her I wished it were a barbed wire fence instead of the torment I experienced.

It is no exaggeration to say that there were many nights my sister and I didn’t know if we were going to live to see daylight. Yet, I refused to let them see me cry. I refused to let him break my will, but I couldn’t keep my mama from breaking my heart. She became like him. She took on his evil ways. In reality, she stopped loving me. She stopped paying me any attention. I felt unloved and unwanted. My little heart shattered into a thousand pieces. It seemed as if it could never be put back together.

I had never known my dad; no one to teach or show me anything. I never had a dad to put me on his knee and bounce me or put me on his shoulders and ride me around. After Mom remarried, I lost her as well. From that time forward, I didn’t know what it was to have a mother anymore, to hug me and tell me she loved me. They broke my heart, but I determined to defend myself at all costs and not let anyone see weakness in me. They would know my anger, but not my weakness.

CHAPTER THREE

I'LL KILL THEM BOTH

The abuse and torment filled me with so much hate and anger that I got into fights all the time. The old folks used to talk about people who fight at the drop of a hat. I was the guy who dropped the hat. Everybody I saw looked like they wanted me to hit them, and I didn't want to disappoint. I refused to let anyone think I was weak. I would fight even if the guy was twice my size, and I knew I couldn't win. It may sound crazy, but even if I lost, I enjoyed hurting someone in the process.

At school, I was in the principal's office more than he was! I should have been the principal. When he saw me in the office, he stopped asking me why I was there and just asked who I was fighting this time. I know it doesn't happen this way today, but we would get whippings in those days, even at school. He would tell me to bend over, and then he took a considerable board with holes in it and laid it, not so gently, to my backside. Wham! When you got hit with that board, you would stand up with each whack. I should've been seven feet tall as much as he raised me up. I'd cuss, and he would give me a few more whacks with the board trying to teach me to change my vocabulary. But cussing is all I knew, and by this time, I was pretty good at it.

The lack of love, the rejection, and the cruel treatment fed an increasingly growing hatred in my childish heart. Adding to it was the very real misery of hunger. I've heard people say that they've never gone hungry, and I'm so glad. My mom and step-dad used most of their money to buy alcohol. They drank the cash up and filled their bellies with food, but we children went for days without food. There were times we were so hungry, we didn't know if we could survive. I'm not exaggerating; we didn't know if we'd make it or not. We hunted glass bottles to turn in for money so we could buy a little food. Sometimes, we even went through trash cans to see if we could find something to eat. I'm not proud of some things we ate, but we did what was necessary to survive. I hope you don't know what I'm talking about, and I pray you never have to experience it personally.

I remember when he and Mama went out of town for several days and dropped us off at his parent's place. It soon became clear that his pain and cruelty came from them. They locked us up in a small trailer where they typically kept hunting dogs. The dog's poop and pee were cleaned, but the place was still infested with fleas and ticks. They forced us inside and locked the door behind us. It was the middle of summer, and it was so hot. We tried to escape, but there was no way out. I can't explain the tormenting feeling of being locked in a trailer with fleas and ticks in stifling summer heat. The door had just enough holes cut in it to allow sufficient airflow to prevent us from suffocating. But it was barely enough. We sat as close to the door as possible, putting our faces to the holes, seeking any relief we could find.

They kicked us back when they opened the door to bring us water and food. It isn't very comfortable to tell you, but it is true: they put our water in the dog bowls and only gave us stale bread to eat. Somebody said, "I would never drink that!" I didn't want to either. But, after a while, you do what you must do to survive. It was drink it or die from dehydration. So, I reached down and got as much as I could in my hand and licked it up. We hated it, and my sister cried. But we choked down the stale bread they had thrown in. It was disgusting, but at least it was food.

I can never forget looking at my sister and saying, "One day! One day I will be big enough to kill them. I'm going to kill him and watch the blood drain from his body. And Mama, too. I'm going to watch the blood flow from her body. I'll enjoy every drop that comes out of them. I want them to die in as much pain and agony as possible."

Linda looked at me with pleading eyes and said, "Larry, they're beating us and tormenting us, but please don't let them make out of you what he is. He wants to make you like him. Don't let him do it! Don't go that way, please. You're scaring me!"

With rage in my voice, I shook my head, "You mark

it down, someday I'll kill him!"

I hated both of them more than I can describe. I hated him for what he was doing. I hated her for allowing it! All I thought about was vengeance. I dreamt of the day when I could get the ultimate revenge! I can't tell you all he did to me. I don't want to remember all of it. It was abuse in the most horrible fashion. I vowed to make him pay. And, even though she was my Mama and I loved her, I vowed to make her pay as well.

One night, when I was nine, I made good on my vow. Well, I tried. It was another night of drunken rage. He had beaten us, and I was bleeding badly. After they fell into a drunken sleep, I went into the kitchen and grabbed the largest butcher knife I could find. I snuck as quietly as I could into their bedroom. I was shaking, both from fear and rage. Something in me knew I shouldn't do it, but the hatred and desire for revenge moved me forward. They didn't wake as I snuck over to his side of the bed and stood over him. I knew I was small and didn't have the arm strength to drive the knife in deep enough, so I fell on him with the knife aimed at his chest. I hoped my body weight would help drive the knife deep enough to kill him.

I don't know what woke him, but he rolled out of my way, and the knife plunged into the mattress as I fell. My mom screamed as he pushed her out of the bed, and jumped out on the opposite side. I turned to run, but he grabbed me and flung me down to the floor, and gave me the worst beating of my life. I thought he was going to kill me. At that moment, I wanted him to kill me. He grabbed the knife, pulling it out of the mattress and cursing me.

Turning to me with the blade firmly in hand, he spoke in a guttural tone, "I'll split your throat."

Hurting, bleeding, and shaking, I glared at him. "Go ahead! I don't want to live, anyway."

I thought he might do it, and although fearful, death seemed better than the life I was experiencing.

Enjoying Life In The Early Days

He restrained himself and looked coldly at me. "You'll never kill me, boy, but I will kill you! One more time like this and I'll kill you for sure!"

I crawled out of the room to my own, vowing to myself that I would outlive him. Telling myself that I would live at least long enough to get my vengeance. I would live to grow big enough to make him pay for what he was doing to my sisters and me. The day would come when they would both pay dearly! They would pay with their lives!

CHAPTER FOUR

LOOKING FOR JOHN WAYNE

Obviously, we never went to church. Even though God had performed miracles for our family, Jesus was not welcome in our home. We couldn't even say God or Jesus unless we were using the names as curses. I can only recall being in a church one time in my childhood. When I was eight years old, I heard about a church in our neighborhood having Vacation Bible School. I wasn't interested in religion, and I sure wasn't interested in the school aspect, but I was very interested in their advertised refreshments. I heard they were going to have sandwiches, cupcakes, and Kool-Aid.

I didn't ask permission to go. I simply roamed the streets as I wanted. They didn't care. But that night, when I got home, Mama somehow knew that I'd been to church.

"Boy, did you go to that church?"

"Yes, Mama I did."

She gave me an angry sneer and asked, "Did you find out anything about that Jesus?"

"Yes, Mama. I did."

She smirked, "Really? What did you find out about Jesus?"

I smiled. "I found out that he's got good sandwiches, cupcakes and Kool-Aid, and I ate them for him today. I'll go back tomorrow and eat the rest of them."

She looked hard at me, but she didn't forbid me to go back. "That's alright. But don't bring any of that Jesus stuff into this house. Don't you dare bring it in this house!"

Then, as she moved into another room, she shoved me. She pushed me back out of her way and away from her. I wanted so badly for her to put her arms around me and hug me. I longed for her to tell me she loved me. But she never did.

Well, I went back every night to eat Jesus' food and drink His Kool-Aid. The food was amazing to me. At least that week, I got plenty to eat. I had no way of knowing that the things I heard them share about Jesus got deep into my soul. It was seed going into the soil of my heart, and one day something good would result. God was working for my good, despite the hell they forced me to live in.

Two years later, the seed of the gospel blossomed into fruit.

I was ten years old, and once again, they spent all their money on whiskey, beer, and whatever else. It was a regular occurrence. They drank it up. When they realized they were out of money, my stepdad encouraged Mama to call up one of her aunts. He figured she would give them money if she thought they would buy food for the kids. He was right. Aunt Elsie possessed a soft spot for children. By this time, a recent addition was in the family. My little brother, David, had been born.

She had us a meal prepared when we arrived, and boy was it good! That day, I thought she was the best cook in the world. Later in life, after I ate at my future wife's home, I came to realize that Aunt Elsie wasn't really a great cook. But to a starving boy, she was amazing!

After the meal, the adults went out on the front porch to talk. They were working Aunt Elsie to get as much money from her as they could. In reality, she wasn't an easy mark, but known to be tight with her money. But that's why they brought us along. She could see we were malnourished, and it was our apparent neglect that moved her to help.

She said, "If you'll buy those kids something to eat, I'll give you the money. Don't use it to drink. Get them something to eat." They promised they would and that they would take better care of us with the money, but, of course, they were lying.

Well, while they were talking outside, I made my way inside to watch some TV. I was looking for anything with some violence. I wanted to see some fighting, shooting, and killing. I lived for revenge but I wasn't big enough to get it yet. However, while I waited, watching violence helped to feed the anger that constantly smoldered deep within me. Getting to watch it fed the dream of life to see them pay for all they did. One day I would get my revenge!

Oral Roberts Under The Big Tent

Back in those days, televisions didn't have remotes, and there were only three channels. When I turned the TV on, I saw a massive tent with people streaming into it. It caught my attention, so I sat down, thinking maybe it was a circus. I thought I would watch it for a minute and then try to find a western or war movie where John Wayne always makes the bad guy pay!

Something about the music arrested my attention as I sat down. I'd heard nothing quite like it before. I later found out it was the sound of a Hammond B-3 organ, and the song they were singing is one I can never forget. "Where the healing waters flow, Where the joys celestial glow, Oh, there's peace and rest and love, Where the healing waters flow!" And then they introduced Oral Roberts. He walked out and took the microphone in hand and started preaching.

When I realized it wasn't a circus, and he was going to preach, I tried to get up to turn the channel. I didn't want them to come in and catch me listening to something religious. I figured we would get beaten again tonight anyway, but I didn't want to add a reason for extra brutality. But as I tried to get up, I couldn't. Something held me down. I couldn't move. I know some will scoff at this and say it didn't happen this way. But I was there when it happened, and I guess I ought to know! I didn't know what it was then, but the Holy Ghost held me down in my seat, and I couldn't change the channel.

Oral Roberts preached.

"Jesus loves you. He died for your sins. The Son of God gave His life for you on the old rugged cross. But on the third day He rose from the dead. He lives! And He will love you when nobody else loves you. If your Mama doesn't love you, and your daddy doesn't love you, and you feel like nobody loves you. If you feel you have nothing and no one, Jesus loves you! He will forgive you of your sins and save you."

I didn't understand all he was saying, but I thought, "Could it be true? Could there be someone who would truly love me? I've had no one to care for me or love me. Is there somebody that really would love me?"

As I listened, I felt something warming in my chest. Hope sprang up.

"Maybe it is true. Perhaps I am loved."

Then the preacher said, "If you'll believe in your heart and confess with your mouth, you'll be saved. Repeat this prayer after me and Jesus will save you."

I repeated a short and simple prayer.

"O Lord, be merciful to me a sinner. Come into my heart and save me from my sins. I repent and receive Christ as my personal Savior. I will live for Him forever by His grace. Amen."

Even though I didn't understand, I spoke the words after him. And it happened like Oral Roberts said it would. Jesus came into my life. He saved me. I felt love like I'd never known. I felt it come into me. Something lifted off of me, and I was happy! The icy, angry grip of hatred released my heart. I was freed. Such gladness filled my heart. I didn't know what to do. I ran outside and grabbed my mama.

"Mama, Mama!"

She responded by pushing me away from her, "What is it now, you little brat?"

"Mama, I'm saved."

She scoffed. "Saved? Where did you hear that? That's religious nonsense. What were you watching? If there was such a thing, you couldn't receive it. You're the meanest child that ever lived on God's earth. You are too mean to be saved."

She looked at the others and said, "Whatever this is, it will blow over by morning! Trust me."

Well, I've got good news for you. Praise God, it didn't blow over by the following day! It still hasn't blown over, but it is blowing up! It's exploded all over this nation and other nations of the world. And the best is yet to come. Jesus gloriously saved me. I didn't need to understand it, but just needed to believe. Faith came by the preaching of His word. Hope sprang up and gave birth to faith. I believed and, thank God, I received. I received the life of Jesus and became a new creation, just like the Bible says in 2 Corinthians 5:17, "Therefore, if anyone is in Christ, he is a new creation; old things have passed away; behold, all things have become new."

A wonderful change took place in me, and, praise God, I'm still living in the victory these many decades later.

CHAPTER FIVE

WHO'S TALKING

After Mama pushed me away and told me it would all blow over, I still tried to hug her because what was in me felt so new and so good. But she pushed me away again. "Don't touch me, you little brat. You'll be in trouble and fighting by the morning."

I didn't know what not fighting had to do with being saved, but at the moment, I didn't want to fight anybody because the love of God was so real to me. I only wanted to love everybody!

That night my new life in Jesus experienced a great test. They did what they always did and used the money for alcohol. Once again, my stepdad got crazily drunk. That night he got in such a horrible drunken state that we didn't know if we'd live to see the light of day. He beat us until we could only lie trembling against the wall. We shook all night and only fell into a fitful sleep when he passed out. The torment and pain were indescribable.

The following day, I woke up to my little half-brother still crying. I don't know if he cried all night or not. I assume he slept at some point, but I went to sleep with him crying and woke up to him crying. We had no food in the house. There was no milk for him to drink, and the little guy was hungry. We were all hungry. The meal from the afternoon before was now just a pleasant memory. I had grown accustomed to the hunger, but I hated to see little David have to go through it.

I got dressed and left the house. They didn't care where I went. I could go anywhere and do anything. It didn't matter to them unless I got into trouble that might get them into trouble. Otherwise, they didn't care if I ever came back. I had no one to help me. No one did anything for me, nothing at all. So I learned to fight for whatever I could get. I learned to fight back. I made a vow to myself that no one would ever abuse me again. No one would ever bully me again!

I thought, "Someday, I'll be 6' 9" and 290 pounds of pure muscle."

In the past, I dreamt of getting my stepdad in my arms and squeezing him until his eyes popped out of his head. But today was different. I was different. Oh, I would still fight, but the hate that had driven me so mercilessly was no longer there. I was learning the change that Jesus brings.

Not heading anywhere in particular, I started walking down the road. My little brother's cries overwhelmed me. He was so pitiful, and I wished I could help him. As I walked, I could hear his cry echoing through my mind, chasing me down.

A prayer rose out of my heart, "Jesus, Jesus, who

Oral Roberts talked about. I don't know how to pray. If you can hear me, I've been hungry a lot of times, and I'm hungry right now. But my little brother's dying, he's dying. Oral Roberts said to pray. I don't know how to pray, but is there some way you could give us some money, some way to get him some milk? Don't let him die. Please don't let him die."

Teaching Generations To Hear God!

At that moment, I heard a voice. I'm not kidding. I heard a voice with my ears not just in my mind. It frightened me. My heart started racing and my palms grew sweaty. It almost scared me to death! I thought someone had snuck up behind me. I jerked around to see, but there was no one there. I looked right and left, but didn't see anyone. Nervously I laughed, shook my head, and started walking again.

Then I heard the voice again, "Look down my son, for I have provided for thee."

I looked down, and there at my foot was a twenty-dollar bill. Glory to God! It was truly miraculous. God had provided. As you read this, $20 may not seem like much, but back in 1959 it was a lot of money. In fact, at the time of this writing, it would be a value of a little over $180. It was a fortune!

I picked it up and looked up toward Heaven. "Wow. Thanks!"

I held it tight in my hand and headed to the little store in our neighborhood. I got a half-gallon of milk, a loaf of bread, some peanut butter, and some strawberry jelly. And I got myself a Pepsi and a Moon Pie. I'm telling you, I thought I was the wealthiest guy in the entire world. I mean, I had a bag full of groceries, drinking a Pepsi and devouring a delicious Moon Pie. Plus, I had some money left over, which I hid in my pocket and headed home.

When I got back home, Mama looked at me suspiciously. "Where did you steal the money to get this stuff, you thieving brat?"

"Mama, I didn't steal it. Truly, I didn't."

She glared at me angrily.

"I'll bust your mouth, you lying brat. We don't have any money and you certainly don't have any money. So, tell me, where did you get the money for all this?"

I told her I found it on the street while I was walking. I didn't dare tell her that God spoke to me and put it at my feet. She would've beaten me for sure. But as she unpacked the bag, it appeared my answer satisfied her.

Then came the question I was hoping to avoid.

"Do you have any more?"

I'm telling you, twenty-four hours earlier, I would

have lied so fast it would make you dizzy. Before praying and giving my life to Jesus, I would have said, "No, Mama. I have no more money. I used it all to buy what I brought home." But now I knew I couldn't lie. I didn't understand why I couldn't lie, but I instinctively knew that I couldn't. So I told her it was in my sock. She made me hand it all to her and went into another room to hide it. I was sad that she now had the rest of the money, since they would likely use it for more alcohol. Yet, I was still happy! I mean, thrilled! God had answered my prayer! My little brother had something to eat. I got to drink my Pepsi Cola and eat a Moon Pie! Glory to God! But most of all, I was excited that God had heard and answered my prayer for help! Hallelujah!

CHAPTER SIX

A NEW HOME

The following day, I got up and started walking the streets again. As I walked, I prayed.

"Jesus, that Oral Roberts talked about, I don't know how to pray."

You know, sometimes, I think we need to get back to that place: the place where we know it isn't our ability or knowledge, so we don't lean on our understanding, but simply pray with a desperate, child-like faith. Remember, you don't need fancy words. Your fancy words do not influence God. A prayer of faith influences Him out of the heart of someone desperate for Him.

That Tuesday morning, I spoke aloud as I walked. "I don't know how to pray. But, Jesus? Oral Roberts said we need to go to church. I want to meet you and Oral Roberts there. Please make a way for me to go to church."

I was just a very unlearned ten-year-old and simply prayed what was in my heart. When I got back home, it wasn't over five minutes before the phone rang. It was Aunt Elsie, Mom's aunt, whose house we were at a couple of days earlier.

She said to Mom, "You know my husband is dead and I'm lonely. Would you let me take Larry and raise him?"

I'll never forget how Mom answered her. "You think you can handle that little mean devil? He's the meanest child on the face of the earth. He's always in trouble. We continually get called to the school because he cusses and fights everybody. He's constantly in trouble. There's no way you can handle him."

"Well, please let me try. I need someone. I understand you'll miss him."

My mama's answer hurt me. "Oh, I don't care if you take him. I could not care less. I don't want him. If you can handle him, you're welcome to him."

I hope you never hear your mama say those kinds of things about you. It felt like a knife thrust into my heart. Oh God, it hurt! I felt the impact of the rejection like a gut punch that leaves you feeling nauseous. But I wouldn't let them see me cry. I'd made up my mind that no matter what they did to me, they would never see me cry. They whipped me. They beat me. But somehow, I never let them see me cry. I didn't know then that it was forming me in the mold of what I hated the most. I was becoming like him! Yet the Lord, in His mercy was watching over me even then.

Mama grabbed what clothes I had and threw them in the paper bag I'd used to bring groceries home the day before. All it took was a grocery bag for my belongings. I only had two shirts, two pairs of pants, a couple of pairs of underwear, and maybe a toothbrush and comb. It's funny to think of now. My clothes were so pitiful that my pants were full of holes. They were embarrassing then, but with today's fashions, they would not only be in style but worth some real money. I didn't know that I was wearing expensive pants! I thought mine were worn-out jeans. Times have certainly changed.

She took the packed bag and slammed it into my chest. "Come on, boy. I'm going to get rid of you."

Trembling, I asked, "Mama, why don't you love me?"

She just looked at me with disgust. "Shut up!"

We drove over to Aunt Elsie's house without a lot of talking. I sat in the back seat, looking out the window and resolving not to let my stepdad or mom see me cry. My palms were sweating, and I couldn't stop shaking, but I did my best to hide it. As hellish as my life was, it was still frightening to think of change. All I knew was torment. Now, I was entering the unknown. More than anything, I was facing the harsh reality that even my mother didn't care for me. I knew it, but now there was no denying it. The realization struck me so hard that I couldn't stop the shaking.

As we pulled up to her house, they unceremoniously honked the horn. She didn't immediately appear, so he laid on the horn. She came hurriedly out now, showing both aggravation and nervousness. Aunt Elsie opened the gate and gave me a welcoming motion. I stepped off the sidewalk onto the porch and turned to look back at the car. In my nervousness, I forgot to grab my bag. Mama swore and threw it at me.

She looked at Aunt Elsie and said, "Well, here he is. See what you can do with him."

She didn't say goodbye or anything. No embrace. No love.

She only looked at me long enough to issue a threat. "When I have to come back after you, we're going to give you the beating of your life."

With that, she turned away from me, and they drove off without even a glance my way.

As I watched the car turn the corner, tears sprung to my eyes. Aunt Elsie saw it and put her arm on my shoulder. "Don't cry, Larry."

I turned away from her. "It's the sun."

I didn't want her to think I was crying.

"Well, if you don't cry and if you'll make me a promise, I'll take you to church."

I turned back to her. "To church? Where Jesus and Oral Roberts are?"

Surprised, she said, "What?"

"Where Jesus and Oral Roberts are?"

She shrugged her shoulders. "Well, they say Jesus is there, but I think Oral Roberts is in Oklahoma."

I said, "No. Wherever Jesus is, Oral Roberts will be

there. And I want to meet them. I want to see Jesus, and I want to see Oral Roberts."

I smile now. I know it was silly, but I honestly didn't know any better back then.

We turned to walk into the house, and she said, "If you'll make me a promise..."

I looked up at her expectantly.

"If you'll promise me, you won't fight. You must promise you won't get into any fights this week. If you can keep your promise, I'll take you to church this Sunday."

I wanted to protest, but she led me into the room on the left, just inside the front door. It was huge, with an enormous bed, dressers, and space for a chair. She told me that as long as I was with her, this was my room. I didn't know what to think. My room. A room of my own. I'd been in the home a few times throughout my life, so it wasn't exactly new to me, yet it was all new to me. Wow! My room in my home. I hated to show it, but I couldn't stop the shaking. It all was as frightening as it was exciting.

I looked around and laid my little bag on the bed. Aunt Elsie told me that dinner was waiting, so we headed downstairs to the kitchen. It smelled so good to a starving boy. I don't use the word starving lightly. In fact, after a few days with her, Aunt Elsie took me to see a doctor. The shaking wouldn't stop, and she thought it best to get me checked out. After a thorough examination, the doctor concluded that the physical trauma of malnourishment was causing most of the shaking.

As we headed downstairs to the kitchen, she brought me back to her proposition.

"If you'll promise me, you will not fight this week, I'll take you to church this Sunday."

Celebrating Aunt Elsie's Birthday with My Sister Linda and Aunt Eva

I didn't want to make that promise. I lived to fight! But I reluctantly agreed. I wanted to go to church. This is what I had just prayed for, right? I had asked the Lord to make a way for me to go to church, and amazingly, He did.

So I said, "Alright, I won't fight. I want to see Jesus and Oral Roberts."

She just shook her head, and we ate our first meal together to commemorate the start of a new life for us both. I've eaten many tastier meals since that day, but that first meal at my new home remains some of the best food I've ever eaten.

CHAPTER SEVEN

JESUS AND ORAL ROBERTS

My new home was in what they called the West End. It was one of the toughest neighborhoods in the city. I thought we were tough where I came from, but this was, in some estimations, the roughest part of Asheville. My promise to not fight was tested the day after I arrived. I went for a walk to check out the area and quickly ran into someone that wanted me to bash his head in.

I was minding my business, just looking around when I turned a corner and almost ran into a guy who had "smack me" written all over his face. He was a couple years older than me, and a good bit bigger, but that didn't intimidate me.

He glared at me. "Who are you and what are you doing here?"

There was something about the way he asked that confirmed my immediate assessment.

I rose to my full height and balled my fists together. "What's it any of your business? I live here now. What about you? Who are you and what are you doing here?"

"This is my turf, man. This area belongs to me and my friends, and I don't like little runts ruining the area. I'm going to stomp you all over this ground!"

I felt something rush over me, like scorching water. His words triggered images of my stepdad stomping me. As these memories flashed through my mind, fiery anger came with them.

I could barely see him now through the rage boiling inside me. "I'm going to make your face uglier than it already is. Your mama won't even recognize you. She'll thank me for that. I'm going to knock every tooth you've got out. I'm going to hurt you real bad, boy. Do you understand, punk?"

With clinched fists, I moved toward him but then I remembered - if I hit this guy, I won't get to see Jesus and Oral Roberts this Sunday. I froze in my tracks. I really wanted to hit him so badly. His face needed some rearranging. And I was just the fellow to get it done. But I had a genuine dilemma. I had received the life of Christ. I knew Jesus had changed me, and I needed to keep my promise.

I hated it, but I had no choice.

I hated it but I said, "I can't fight you."

He laughed. "You're afraid!"

I got as close to his face as possible. "No. I'm not afraid of you. You understand that right now. I made a promise. I've got to go see Jesus and Oral Roberts and if I fight, I can't see them. But after I see them on Sunday, I'm going to stomp you! You meet me right here next Monday and I'm going to tear you up!"

He laughed again. "You're stupid, but ok, I'll give you time to get your nerve up. I'll be here, Monday."

We both stomped off in different directions. I really wanted to hit him, even though I felt like it might not be right. Don't judge me, I'd only been a Christian for a few days. I still wanted to hit him, but I wanted to see Jesus and Oral Roberts.

The next Saturday night, my aunt told me to be ready in the morning to go to church. I could hardly sleep any that night. I was up early and quickly got ready to go. By this time she had purchased me some appropriate clothes for church. I can't tell you how excited I was to be wearing new clothes and going to see Jesus and Oral Roberts!

She wasn't as excited as me, so it felt like forever before we finally arrived. The building was extensive and quite nice. I won't mention the denomination, but I will tell you, they were as dead as a graveyard and as cold as a refrigerator. The name should be the First Church of the Ice Box. A six-foot icicle they called the pastor stood behind the podium, and the people were like ice cubes scattered through the building. The only fire I saw in the whole place was burning on the end of the cigarettes they smoked on the front porch.

During the service, Aunt Elsie whispered. "How do you like this?"

My reply confused her. "They don't have it. They

just don't have it."

Trying to be discreet but curious, she asked, "What don't they have?"

I whispered back, probably louder than I realized.

"I don't know exactly, but they sure don't have what Jesus and Oral Roberts have. And where is Jesus, anyway? I don't see Him in here."

She looked around. "I don't see Him, either."

I stood up so I could see the front rows. "And where is Oral Roberts?"

She pulled me down and told me to be quiet.

We picked up our conversation as we drove home. I said, "I don't think that's a real church. At least not like Oral Roberts' church."

She chuckled. "I think I know what you're wanting. Oral Roberts is one of those tongue talking Pentecostals. I'll take you to that kind of church next week if you'll promise not to fight."

"Oh, I can't promise you that. I've got a fight scheduled for tomorrow."

She informed me that if I fought the next day, or any day that week, she wouldn't take me to church the following Sunday. As much as I hated it, I once again agreed. I just had to see Jesus and Oral Roberts.

Well, the next morning I ran into that guy, that fellow, that punk. Sorry, but that was how I felt then.

He sized me up. "So, you ready to fight?"

I clinched my teeth. "Not today!"

Oh my, did that set him off! He jumped at me and told me I was just a big chicken and afraid to fight him. His words triggered a deeper explosion in me.

I felt that heat flush all over me and said, "I told you I couldn't fight until I see Jesus and Oral Roberts and I didn't get to see them yet. I wish I had, so I could stomp your face into the ground!"

School Photograph 1954

He moved closer, and I stepped to meet him. But somehow I held myself and told him I was going to the holy roller church this weekend to see Jesus and Oral Roberts and then I'd take care of him.

He laughed. "A what church? What is a holy roller?"

I didn't have a clue myself what it was, but that is what my aunt called it.

I didn't want him to know I didn't know either.

I rolled my eyes. "Don't you know anything?"

I was the one about to find out.

CHAPTER EIGHT

A GHOST

The following Sunday, I got up excited to go to church, but my aunt wouldn't go that morning. I don't know why, but she waited until Sunday night. It seemed, to my ten-year-old brain, that she was purposefully trying to frustrate me. I got upset and would've pitched a fit, but, not wanting to jeopardize going that night, I controlled my tongue. Man, it seemed like the day went on forever, but finally night came and we left for church.

This church was literally just down the hill from the house, so we walked. It's crazy, but living that close, we were still late! Aunt Elsie didn't believe in being on time for anything, anywhere. She liked to arrive fashionably late, so by the time we got there, the service was in full swing. The building had windows along the front so as we walked up we could see inside. Wow! There were a lot of people inside. Some were jumping up and down, some were shaking, and some were dancing.

I thought, "My goodness, what is this?"

I looked at my aunt. "I'm not going in there. This isn't a church, it's a beer joint."

She laughed. "This isn't a beer joint!"

She didn't convince me. I knew drunk. I'd witnessed the erratic behavior of those under the influence all my life. Almost everybody I could see in there looked drunk to me!

I peered through the window and saw this little woman moving from person to person, and it looked like she was knocking them down. She wasn't five feet tall but big men would stand in front of her and when she touched them with her hand, many of them fell, shaking to the ground.

I looked up at Aunt Elsie and told her again, "We can't go in there! You see what that woman is doing to those big men? She'll kill us!"

It looked like she was using some kind of martial arts on them. I thought maybe she knew Judo or Karate or something. I shook my head and refused to go inside. She assured me she would take care of me, but I still wasn't convinced.

Aunt Elsie looked at me and said, "Listen, you can run, can't you?"

I thought about it. She was right. I could actually run quite fast.

I nodded.

"Ok. We will sit in the back where we can slip out real quick if we need to. But I want to see what is going on."

So we snuck in and sat as close to the back as

possible. She motioned me into the row, and as I moved in, she moved in behind me, blocking my exit. Well, it didn't take long for my fear to become my reality. The Bible says what Job feared came upon him, but what I feared came after me! That little preacher woman walked right back to where I was.

She looked at me and pointed her finger in my direction. "Son."

I looked around, hoping there was another son close by, but I realized I was the only son left in that section.

She said, "You, son. Do you want to be saved?"

I stuttered. "No, ma'am."

"You don't want to be saved?"

"No ma'am. Jesus and Oral Roberts saved me two weeks ago. Is Jesus here?"

"Oh, yes!" she replied.

"Well, can I see Him?"

"You will!"

I smiled, and she smiled. Then I shocked her with my next question.

"Where's Oral Roberts?"

She looked puzzled. "I think he's in Oklahoma."

I knew nothing about church, so I assumed Oral Roberts would be there when I showed up. Of course, I now know that Oral Roberts or anyone of us, can't be in every church, but thank God, Jesus is always present when His Church gathers!

She then asked me the strangest question of my ten-year-old life.

"Do you want the Holy Ghost?"

I shook my head no! No way! I didn't want a ghost. I had no clue what holy meant, but I knew I sure didn't want a ghost.

"Does Oral Roberts have this Holy Ghost?"

She smiled. "Oh, yes!"

"Does Jesus have it?"

She nodded and again said, "Yes."

So, I stretched my hands out to her and said, "Okay, I'll take it."

I had no idea what it was, but if Jesus and Oral Roberts had it, then I wanted it.

Sis. Porche grabbed my hand and pulled me out of the pew and forward to the front of the church. She took me to the visiting preacher and asked him to pray for me. He went through the same questions, and I answered them the same way.

"If Jesus and Oral Roberts have it, then I want it, too!" Then, I stretched my hands out so he could give it to me and I could put the Holy Ghost in my pocket and go home.

He smiled. "Son, you don't have to understand in order to receive. Just believe and open your heart."

Then he reached his hand toward me to pray.

I don't know if his hand ever touched my head. Suddenly, I couldn't stand. I fell backwards, and it felt like someone picked me up and gently laid me down on a feather bed. My chest was on fire. My tongue felt thick and on fire as I lay there, shaking. When I got up, I was as drunk as the rest of the folks in the room, and I was talking in a language I didn't know. I'd never felt so good in all my life. Actually, I think I got a little drunker!

People were praising God around me.

"He's got it! He received the baptism of the Holy Ghost."

I got so drunk I had to have a designated walker. Remember, we just lived up the hill from the church, but I needed someone to help get me home. They helped me navigate the walk as I continued shaking and quaking all the way up the hill. I didn't come out from under the influence of the Holy Ghost even when I got into the house. I continued speaking in tongues all the way until I went to bed and eventually fell asleep.

I woke the next morning to the sound of my aunt knocking on the door. She asked me what I wanted for breakfast. When I opened my mouth to answer, it happened all over again. I started shaking and speaking in tongues. It was awesome. It felt wonderful, but I got scared. I thought to myself, I can't go through life shaking and unable to speak English. When I became afraid, it stopped, and I went to eat my breakfast.

But when I realized that the sweet power of the Lord's anointing had lifted off of me, I ran back to my room and fell on my face praying, "Jesus, Jesus please don't take this Holy Ghost from me."

In answer to my cry, His sweet presence washed over me again, and I spent hours praising Him as I enjoyed the sweet baptism in the Holy Spirit.

Of course, I didn't know the Bible yet. I didn't know the great truths concerning the Holy Spirit and His ministry as our Great Helper, but thankfully, the Lord worked with me where I was and planted me in a Bible-believing church where I could grow.

I guess I should tell you the rest of the story about the gang leader who wanted to fight me.

The week following my being baptized in the Holy Ghost, he and a couple of his cronies stopped me on the street.

I really didn't go to meet him. With the blessedness of my experience with God, I forgot about our scheduled appointment. But he remembered.

"Have you seen your Jesus and the other guy so you can fight me?"

Here's the thing. After receiving the Holy Ghost, I didn't really want to fight him anymore, but I didn't know how to get out of it, especially with his buddies there.

I silently prayed. "Lord, what do I do?"

And the Lord answered me. "Raise your hands and praise me, son!"

So, I did. I raised both hands and lifted my eyes toward Heaven and started praising God. I began quietly, but soon my voice was booming. Within seconds the sweet and powerful Spirit of God moved on me and I started shaking, speaking in tongues, and dancing. I got so happy in Jesus I entirely forgot about those guys. When I finally looked around, I couldn't find them anywhere! The Lord helped me out and blessed me in the process. I am so glad I got acquainted with the Ghost of God! He is the best Helper ever!

Years later, I had a conversation with the guy who wanted to fight me. We were much older, of course, and we reminisced about that time.

It was a great opportunity to find out where they disappeared to that day.

"Where did you guys go?"

"When you started speaking in tongues and dancing we ran because my mama told me that crazy people will hurt you and you looked crazy."

We laughed. Then he said, "You know, Larry, we came to respect you in the neighborhood. When you preached, we'd sneak down to the church and listen to you from outside. We didn't understand it but we felt something when you were preaching."

He told me he put the word out to everyone in the neighborhood that if they bothered me, they would have to answer to him. No wonder it got so good for me. I didn't have to fight like I used to because God used a guy who wanted to fight me to become my protector!

The Asheville Revival Center

It always pays to obey God, regardless of how foolish you may look or feel. The most foolish thing you could do is refuse to yield to the Holy Ghost. Be smart and yield yourself today and always.

CHAPTER NINE

A ROOFTOP EXPERIENCE

When God wants to enlarge your world, He often brings people into your life who will stretch your horizons. He certainly did for me. I began regularly attending the church just down the hill where I received the Holy Ghost. Everyone needs a home church, and the Lord placed me there at the Asheville Revival Center on 10 Roberts Street.

Not only did I get baptized in the Holy Spirit there, but I also got water baptized. It was winter now, and I still knew little. I didn't know about water baptism yet, but one night they preached about it and were baptizing some people in the baptistry. As I listened to the message, I realized water baptism was necessary for all who follow Jesus. I wanted in on it. Since I didn't know water baptism was happening, I didn't come prepared with a change of clothes. But I refused to let that stop me. I joined the line and got baptized. Oh my, it was a glorious moment! Well, not everything was glorious! Being so young, I didn't take the weather into account. It was below freezing that night. And I had to walk home. By the time I got up the hill, my clothes were stiff. Frozen! You would have laughed, watching me try to get out of them. But thank God, the fire of the Holy Ghost was burning strong inside my spirit.

Not long afterwards, I met a tall man with jet black hair that touched the top of his dress shirt collar, who would change my life. He and his wife came to conduct revival services regularly there at the Revival Center. When I first saw him, I thought he might be Jesus. I'd never been close to anyone with such authority, such power, and the manifestation of the presence of God. I saw with my own eyes genuine miracles take place when he prayed. And the power of the Lord was tangible in the services he led.

I remember looking at him and asking, "Jesus?"

He shook his head. "No, son. I'm H. Richard Hall."

"Oh. I thought you might be Jesus. Could you tell me if I'll ever get to see Jesus, or ever get to see Oral Roberts?"

He looked at me with his piercing, dark eyes. "You'll see Jesus, son."

When I first met Bro. and Sis. Hall, as they were affectionately called, I couldn't have imagined the impact they would have on my life. I couldn't imagine that one day I would serve in ministry with them, as a pastor and member of the executive board of United Christian Church and Ministerial Association. I was simply in awe of the Jesus that I sensed and witnessed in them. Please understand, I certainly learned that he wasn't Jesus. I realized he wasn't perfect. But I came to know him as a tremendous prophet of God, like a Moses to our generation. In many ways, he became to me like the dad I never had in my life. In fact, when I was thirteen, Bro. Hall asked my mom for permission for he and Sis. Hall to adopt me as their own. But she refused. Yet, even though that wasn't the path my life took, I still looked to Bro. and Sis. Hall as a spiritual dad and mom, and I'm forever grateful for their influence and impact on my life.

All of Bro. Hall's services were amazing, but one particular Sunday afternoon service is most memorable. That service changed my life forever. I was 11 years old. As Bro. Hall was preaching, a deep move of the Lord came into the building. He pointed his finger toward the audience and prophesied.

"There are seventeen people in this building right now who are receiving an ordination to preach. If you'll get out of here, the higher you get, the more God will pour His Spirit on you."

I ran outside and looked at the telephone pole, thinking I would climb it, but quickly decided it wouldn't work, so I ran behind the church.

I stood there looking at the high rounded roof, thinking, "If I could just get up there."

While I was looking and trying to figure out a way up on the roof, someone spoke from behind me.

"Son, what do you want?"

I turned and saw a big man, maybe the tallest man I've ever seen. To be honest, I'm not sure if it was a man or an angel. I can't recall ever seeing him before or after that moment.

"Son, what do you want?"

"The prophet of God said to get outside. He said God called seventeen of us to preach, and the higher we go, the more anointing we will receive from the Lord. I want on top of this church!"

The stranger said, "You think you can handle it?"

"Yes sir! I just need help to get up there."

With that, he grabbed hold of me and lifted me up on the edge of the roof. I pulled myself up and made it to the top. Professional roofers have heard my story and marveled because the grade of the roof is too steep for anyone to walk on without special shoes and ropes. David said, "...by my God have I leaped over a wall." (Psalm 18:29) By the Holy Ghost I ran, shouting and preaching all over that roof. I opened my mouth and the Word of God flowed out. I didn't really know much Bible yet. Certainly not like it was coming out of me. The Spirit of God was declaring the Word of God powerfully out of a little boy's mouth!

One day, many years later, Bro. Hall asked me to sit with him for a moment because he wanted to talk with me.

"I'm going to say something to you, I've never said

to any other man, and you weren't a man when it happened."

I looked at him, wondering what he was referring to.

"Son, you were just a boy when you took all of my crowd. I had to come listen to you preach because everyone emptied the building to hear you preach from the top of it. I had to come listen to you. And son, they can't blame your long preaching on me. The first time you preached, you preached over an hour. You took the whole service. Now, son, you started on top don't you ever go to the bottom."

H. Richard and Amelia Hall

After that, God used me in powerful ways. As a kid preacher they invited me to preach in a variety of places, some small and some large, but in every place the Spirit of the Lord moved powerfully! I remember one occasion when I was just thirteen. They invited me to preach in a large gathering in Hickory, NC. Hundreds were present. On Saturday night, I noticed a boy in a wheelchair, paralyzed from the waist down. The Lord spoke to me to go pray for him.

He said, "I'm going to heal him right now."

I left the platform and went down to him. He had braces on his legs and I asked his dad and mom to take them off. They agreed but not because of their faith. They told me he had never walked and wouldn't.

I looked directly at them. "The Lord said, 'He's going to walk tonight!'"

The young man turned around to his mom and dad. "See, I told you so!"

What I didn't know was that on Wednesday of that week, he was sitting in his wheelchair in front of a large window, watching across the street as some boys were playing. They were running with a ball, climbing trees, roughhousing with each other, and other normal things guys do.

As he set there wishing he could join in, the Lord spoke to him and he turned and told his mom.

"Mom, God's going to let me run and play like those guys across the street."

With a tear sliding down her cheek, she walked over and laid her hand on his shoulder. "I know, son. When you get to heaven one day, you'll be able to do all of that and more."

"After this Saturday, I'll be able to do it all."

Her heart shuttered with fear because it sounded like he was going to die on Saturday.

"Mama, not in Heaven, but here. God said He is

going to heal me this Saturday night. I'll be able to run this Saturday."

I didn't know any of that. All I knew is that God told me to pray for him and He would heal him!

This kid was about the same age as me, but under the anointing of the Holy Ghost, I took him by the hand and said, "Son, rise and walk. Be healed in the name of Jesus!"

At thirteen, my voice was squeaky, not powerful, but he got up! He was shaky at first and they reached out to help him, but he stopped them. He insisted on doing it himself. As he acted on his faith, the Holy Spirit touched his body, and we watched as he started walking. He struggled up and then he started walking. Then he ran. He ran around the building until he was out of breath from the exertion. I remember it like it was yesterday! I'll never forget the gigantic smile on his and his mama's face as they embraced each other.

What a moment it was! Many other wonderful things happened that night as the spirit of the Lord responded to the faith of the people. As they reached out to the Lord, they discovered that He was reaching out to them. It was glorious!

I need to tell you, though, that when you obey the Lord, the enemy will do all he can to stop you. And often he'll use people in your own family and those you love the most. I'll tell you in a couple of chapters about the call I received from my mother threatening to blow my brains out if I didn't stop preaching. I didn't stop and she couldn't follow through on her threat, because God turned things around.

Those early years were glorious, but I've witnessed God doing greater things since then. And, I believe there are those reading these words who will experience even greater things in God than I have. Get ready! Surrender fully to Christ. Believe and obey His word and you can partner with Jesus in His wonderful plan! The best is yet to come! Before Jesus returns for His people, He is going to manifest His glory through His people as a witness. Multiplied millions are going to come to Christ before the end comes.

CHAPTER TEN

WORTH EVERY MILE

I hope you've noticed that just as the pain of my life was brought on by people, the healing of my life involved people. You see, when the devil wants to destroy your life, he will work through people. But when God redeems and restores, He also works through people. The story of God's great grace in my life isn't complete unless I tell you of a special lady.

As a teenager, I preached to thousands and saw marvelous miracles manifest for the glory of God. The blessing and favor of God was on my life in many ways. The greatest gift came in the most beautiful form. I was fourteen years old when I first saw her in the congregation as I came in and sat down. Her beauty caught my eye and made my teenage heart skip a beat. But as I got to know her, it was more than her physical beauty that attracted me. It was the way she loved Jesus and worshipped God.

Her name was Ramona, and she was a dark-haired beauty. At first, I tried to play the hotshot preacher routine on her. I acted like I didn't notice her or care if she noticed me. It worked on many other girls coming to the church, but it didn't work too well on her. Then I started noticing that other guys were paying her attention. I couldn't have that! Well, I changed my approach and tried a little humility instead of cockiness. Thankfully, it worked! Our eyes met. I smiled shyly, and she smiled back.

I discovered her dad was a preacher who had been in the Free Will Baptist group, like my uncle Bob Self. When Mr. Ingle discovered the baptism of the Holy Ghost, he received the left foot of fellowship. They pushed him out of their movement, and, thankfully; he brought his family down to the Revival Center where I attended. Isn't God good? He and his sweet wife became like a surrogate mom and dad to me.

I didn't get in trouble in school just for fighting. I also got in trouble for not listening. I remember, one day I was so caught up writing Ramona's name out on my paper while I thought about how pretty she was and how much I liked her that I didn't realize the teacher was calling my name. Finally, it broke through in my mind that she was calling on me to answer a question. I don't remember the question, but I remember my incorrect answer, "Ramona!"

The teacher asked, "Who's Ramona?"

I told her she was my girlfriend. Well, Ramona wasn't the answer to the teacher's question that day, but she was the answer to my question!

One day, I summoned the courage to ask her dad if I could have her hand in marriage. Amazingly, he agreed. And my mom agreed to sign as well. I had to have her signature since we were only sixteen years old. (Now, we don't recommend, especially these days, that anyone gets married that young. It wasn't easy for us, but by the grace of God, we've made it.)

Ramona's family lived close to 8 miles from my house, and I didn't have a car. I wasn't even old enough to drive. But I refused to let the distance keep us apart. I walked the miles - not just once a week but multiple times. I would head over after school, eat with them, and then head back home at night. Sometimes I could catch a ride, but many times I ended up walking every mile.

Mr. and Mrs. Larry Nix

You might find this amusing. The reason I discovered I could walk the distance is because I got mad. One Sunday afternoon, after dinner, when we were engaged, Mr. Ingle wanted to take a drive on the Parkway. We pulled over and hiked a short way down a trail.

Ramona suddenly looked at me, "Oh no! Look! My ring isn't on my finger!"

My heart beat over time, and we frantically searched the trail. Everyone got involved in the search, but to no avail. Finally, we had to leave to make it to church that evening.

On the drive down the mountain. Ramona suddenly said, "Oh, look! Here it is!"

She had hidden it in her skirt to play a joke on me. Everyone in the car laughed, including me. But the more I thought about it, the more it made me mad. I got so angry about her tricking me; I jumped out of the car and began walking home as soon as we got back to their house. The distance never crossed my mind. It turned out to be 8 miles, but I didn't care. My feet got terribly blistered, but I was so mad I blamed her for my blisters. I even demanded my ring back. But, it wasn't long before I got over it and made the journey back to her house to make up.

Even though anger was my first motivation, love became my primary motivation. When my feet didn't want to do it, my heart took over and made my feet get to it. She was worth it! Plus, her mama could cook! I mean, cook! After eating her cooking just once, my taste buds and my stomach were now in agreement with my heart. It would take more than lions, tigers, and bears to keep me away. I mean, Mrs. Ingle could cook like nobody's business. And thankfully, Ramona took after her. We certainly know what it is to eat wonderful food at my house.

The food was a great bonus, but it was the joy of being with Ramona that kept me motivated to walk those miles, sometimes through darkness, rain, or snow.

Ramona made my heart go vroom, vroom, vroom. All I could think about was Jesus and Ramona, and sometimes, not in that order!

I often say Ramona married who she thought I was, but if she had known all the struggles from my past, she would have said, "No way. I don't. I won't. I'm out of here!"

Thank God she said, "Yes!"

It certainly hasn't always been easy, and I've given her many reasons to wonder about her yes, but by grace, she stuck with me through it all. She married who she thought I was and got stuck with who I was, but by the grace of God, she stuck with me. I am ever grateful to God for the woman He gave me. You've heard it said that behind every successful man is a surprised mother-in-law. Wait, I mean, a good woman. Both are accurate where I'm concerned!

Thank God, indeed. For 54 years, we've preached the gospel of Jesus together around the nation. We've pastored, planted churches, traveled as evangelists, and raised four wonderful children. Then God blessed us with six incredible grandchildren and two great-grandchildren so far. Plus, dozens and dozens of spiritual children. Any glory for all I've accomplished through the many years goes to the Lord and Ramona. She was undoubtedly worth every mile that I walked!

CHAPTER ELEVEN

I'LL BLOW YOUR BRAINS OUT

When I look back over my life, I am in awe of all the Lord has done. I'm convinced that if He hadn't saved me when He did, I would have killed my step-dad and mom. Who knows who else I would have killed to satisfy my deep thirst for vengeance? I hate to think about how many lives I would have damaged while trying to deal with the damage in my soul. What a tragedy it almost was for me to live my life as a repeat of his. But thank God He rescued me! He saved me and honored me with a calling to reach others.

There is a principle that you need to understand: When you get what you want, you also get what you don't want. When you are blessed you will be attacked. Your breakthrough will arrive with potential setbacks.

The victory and blessings in my life stirred up the devil to attack me again. As I preached and let the Lord work through me, my mom heard about it and reacted in a way that shouldn't have surprised me, but it did. One day, I received a phone call from her.

"You are the greatest embarrassment our family's ever known. I'd rather see you dead than involved in all this crazy religious stuff. I'm coming over there today to blow your brains out."

My heart hurt as my mom drove yet another dagger into it. But I didn't let her know it.

"Mama, you can't kill me. I know you're a good shoot, but you can't shoot me. I am ordained, anointed, and raised up by God to preach His gospel. And Mama, God told me He's going to save my household. That includes you, Mama! Jesus is going to save you Mama!"

She cussed me. "I'll blow your brains out! I'll see you dead! You are an embarrassment to me and I hate that you were ever born."

Then she hung up! Laying the phone down, I went to my room to cry and pray.

"Lord, you heard what she said. Why? I don't understand, but keep her from coming over here with a gun, Lord. I believe the promise you made to me and I will see her saved. Thank you!"

He answered. She didn't show up with a gun, but our terrible relationship became even worse. I wasn't allowed to go around them anymore. They wouldn't come around where we were, and they didn't invite us to the family functions like everyone else. I was now the official outcast of the family and not because of anything evil thing. They hated me so badly because of the work of God in my life.

I really felt like no one loved me, and until Ramona, I had no one. Even my aunt, who rescued me from the hellish house, seemed more motivated by her need for a companion than genuine love for me. I'm so thankful for all she did for me, and I believe she came to love me. In reality, she probably loved me more than I could perceive or receive in those early years. But I remember lying in bed alone at night, holding my pillow and crying myself to sleep. I wept many nights and soaked the pillow with my tears.

I remember one day waking up after a wonderful dream where my mom was hugging me and letting me hug her. She was telling me how much she loved me.

"I love you son, I love you."

When I realized it was still just a dream, my heart fell, and tears came again.

I sobbed. "Lord, if I could just hear her say, 'I love you,' and feel her arms around me, it would be everything to me."

I made a decision that I would believe the word the Lord spoke to me, that as I preached His word and reached others, He would save my mom. The Lord even confirmed this word through a prophetic encounter one night in a revival meeting. I was just a young teenager when a visiting evangelist from another state, in a crowd of hundreds, pointed to me and had me stand.

He prophesied to me about the ministry God had placed within me and then said, "God is going to save your family. If you will be faithful and preach God's word, He is going to save your mama!"

Praying For The Fire of Pentecost!

I rejoiced and made a quality decision to keep preaching and praying in Jesus' name. I would continue to praise Him and obey Him. I had trusted Him with my life, and I would trust Him with hers.

As the years passed, they showed up at places where I was preaching. My heart leaped inside me when I saw them.

"Hallelujah!" I thought, "This is the night Mama will receive the life of Jesus!"

I preached my heart out and did my best to obey the Lord in everything He spoke to me that night. When I made the call to surrender and receive the life of Christ, I pleaded with everything in me. I prayed for everyone in the house who didn't know Jesus in the pardon of their sins, especially Mama. But Mama never responded. I knew that when Mama got saved, she wouldn't hate me anymore. When she knew Jesus like I knew Jesus, I'd finally get to hear her say she loves me and feel her arms around me in a loving embrace. But it never happened in those meetings.

It disappointed me each time, but I never stopped believing in the promise of God. You've got to believe the promise of God. If God doesn't put a date on it, you better not put a time limit on it. If God doesn't tell you when and exactly how it will happen, don't attempt to make it happen the way you imagine it should happen or when you think it should happen. Whatever you do, don't give up on the promise. Trust God! Delay doesn't mean denial. You've got to consider God faithful. He who promised you will bring to pass every promise. Hold on to the promise!

Whatever you are holding onto is what is holding on to you. Those who cling to the promises of God, regardless of how it looks or how long it takes, will see every promise God made you become a reality.

I was about to witness the glory of God's goodness!

CHAPTER TWELVE

MY SON AND YOURS

Though my family hated me and they did not welcome us at family events, they came to respect my relationship with the Lord. My sister, Linda, and Mom knew my prayers got answered.

My mother dealt with a lot of sickness throughout her life. The older she got, the more she struggled. The bad choices really took a toll on her. When she was hospitalized they would call me to let me know. The family wanted me to pray. The Lord graciously heard me and touched her. I can't recall precisely how many times the Lord brought her back from certain death, but time after time, He extended her life. He had made me a promise to save her, and He intended to keep it!

One night, I received a call from my sister Linda that the doctor only gave Mama a couple of hours to live. Linda said if I wanted to see her, I needed to get there as quickly as possible.

When I hung the phone up, I bowed my head in prayer.

"Lord, I'm going to head to the hospital, and I ask you to touch Mama and manifest healing in her body."

I heard His unmistakable voice. Thank God! The ability to hear His voice is worth all the riches of this world. It is more valuable than all earthly knowledge. I may not know much in this world, but I am thankful that I know His voice.

He spoke to me and instructed me not to go that night but to wait until early in the morning to go.

I didn't understand and felt I needed to remind Him that the situation was urgent. "But Lord, they say she doesn't have that long! I have to go now if I am going to see her before she dies."

His response quieted me. "I am God. Don't go until the early morning. Go at the break of day."

I knew I could trust Him.

I knew I must trust Him.

I prayed on and off most of the night, sleeping very little. I got up early while it was still dark to arrive at the hospital just as the sun rose. On the drive to the hospital, I prayed and gave thanks to the Lord for His faithfulness through the years. And though I knew the situation was dire, the peace of God enveloped me wonderfully.

I arrived just before the morning hustle began, so the hospital was still quiet. When I opened the door to Mom's room, three things became evident. First, no one else was in the room but my mom. Second, she looked so pitiful, yet peaceful. Third, I felt the greeting of the sweet Holy Ghost when I stepped into the room. God's presence was tangible.

I could tell that something had happened. Jesus was

present, and things always change when He is in the room! I walked over to the bed. I can still see it in my mind even now. When I share my testimony, there is a sense in which I experience it all over again.

That early morning, as I stood there beside her bed, she looked so pitiful. She looked like a tiny skeleton with skin stretched over it. She weighed maybe 80 pounds, and the stench of the cancer was almost unbearable. Despite all of that, I sensed the tangible presence of the Lord in the room.

Jackie Aiken Weatherford Nix Brown

She opened her eyes and, looking up, recognized me. "Oh, Larry, it's you, son."

She smiled and reached her hand over to take mine.

She told me she had something to say to me I wouldn't believe, then she smiled and said, "Oh yes, you'll believe it because you told me years ago it would happen."

She looked toward the foot of her bed and I saw the sweetest expression of wonder come over her face.

"Larry, somewhere around 3:00 this morning, after everyone had left, and the lights were off, something awakened me suddenly. Before I opened my eyes, I could see the light. The room lit up brighter than any light I'd ever seen. I could make out the image of someone standing at the foot of my bed. At first, I thought it maybe the doctor came in, but it wasn't. It was someone I never thought I would see, and I'll never forget what He looked like."

I interrupted. "Mama, what did He look like?"

Awe was in her voice as she said, "His hair was white as snow. His eyes looked like a flame of fire."

Wow! I know my mama didn't know John's description of Jesus in the book of The Revelation.

I praised the Lord as she continued.

"He looked at me and spoke. 'I am Jesus. I am here to keep My word to My servant; My son, and your son. I've come that I might save you."

As tears streamed down both of our faces (I didn't care if she saw me cry now!), she described how she had cried out for forgiveness. She surrendered and received the life of Christ in that glorious moment.

She described His voice as sounding like thunder, so powerful she said it shook her, as He said, "I forgive your sins."

She smiled, and I smiled too. She now knew He whom my soul loves! My mama now knew Jesus like I knew Jesus! I rejoiced at the faithfulness of God!

Mama broke the moment by saying, "Son, there's

two things I deeply regret about my life. I regret them so badly."

"What, Mama?"

"I regret I didn't receive Jesus before now. Oh, how I've wasted my life. But I know He has forgiven me. I am amazed. He's saved me and I know, I'm going to be with Him."

She shook her head with a look of both awe and sadness. "The other thing, Larry, please understand, I didn't hate you. It was what was in me that hated. I'm so sorry!"

I nodded, and my tears ran fresh. "I forgive you, Mama."

She reached up to me with her bony little arms."I know I don't smell good, son. I'm dying but, could I hold you?"

I had waited, it seemed, all of my life, to hear her say those words. I had cried myself to sleep as a little boy hugging a pillow and pretending it was my mama hugging me. Could she hold me? Tigers or lions couldn't have kept me from letting her hold me!

I reached down and picked up that little body and pulled her close. She wrapped her arms around my neck and held me as I held her. Our flowing tears spoke of the joy and power of God's amazing grace.

She looked up at me and said, "I'll see you in Heaven

now, son. I'll meet you in Heaven, and we'll never be separated again. I love you. I love you!" The explosion that went off in my heart when she said, "I love you," is indescribable.

I'd waited so long and yearned so often to hear those words come out of her mouth. I felt like running up and down the halls of the hospital. We basked in the moment and then I told her I loved her and that I would pray and the Lord would heal her again. She shook her head no and said to me she had to go on. Her time had come.

I objected, but she silenced me.

"Larry, not this time. The Lord told me it was my time to go. But, son, now I'm not afraid to die. I'm ready! He saved me and now I'll get to spend eternity with Him and I'll be with you there as well!"

Sharing my story isn't easy for me. In a sense, I have to relive the rejection and the pain. Some ask me, "Why do you share it then?"

The reason I share it is because you are worth my pain. If my story can help bring just one to know Jesus as I do, it will be worth it all. But thank God, I don't just relive the bad; I get to relive the good as well. And, I know, that all the times I missed on Earth with my mama will be more than made up for in Heaven! She is there now, waiting on me!

Don't ever forget that God is faithful to His word. He will save your family. If you stand for Him, He will stand for you. He is not a man that He should lie, neither the son of man that He should repent. If He says it, He will do it. If He promises it, He will make it happen. You can join the ranks of those in Hebrews 11 who judged God faithful and trusted Him with everything!

He will always come through!

CHAPTER THIRTEEN

MY DESIRE FOR YOU

There are many things I can't tell you. I can't fully describe the beatings, burnings, and stomping, or the hurts, pains, the rejections, and the loneliness. Not only during the years of torment, but afterwards, I still had to deal with uncontrollable shaking, fears, and anger. When the Lord saved me, healing worked instantly in my life, but I've discovered that it is also a process. Some aspects of the healing are still being walked out in my life, but I've learned that God's grace is more than sufficient.

My mom's last request was for me to preach her funeral. It was one of the most difficult things I've ever done. I didn't think I could, but the Lord spoke to me and assured me He was with me and through His anointing, I can do all things! Yet again, the Lord brought me through by His amazing grace and deeply touched all in attendance.

Even my tormentor came to me afterwards and stood trembling.

"Larry, I've never believed in God but God is the only way to describe what I just witnessed and felt as you preached your mama's funeral."

He explained he literally felt himself shaking both on

the inside and outside while I was preaching. And even when he tried to make it stop, he couldn't control what he was feeling.

While he was talking to me, the Lord spoke to me to put my arms around him and tell him I forgave him. What? Tell this horrible man I forgave him for the unspeakable things he did to me, my sister, and the others in my family? I didn't know if I could obey this instruction. I didn't know if I wanted to obey. But within seconds, I surrendered to the Lord and obeyed.

He stood stiffly as I hugged him and told him I forgave him, but a tear escaped and slowly ran down his cheek. He brushed it aside and looked away.

"You can't forgive me after what I did to you."

"If it were just me, you would be right. But Jesus lives in me now. And because Jesus forgave me, I forgive you!"

I reminded him of the gospel. I told him Jesus died for his forgiveness and freedom as much as for anyone else's. I encouraged him to receive the life of Christ. Sadly, he shook his head no.

"I can't receive forgiveness after all I've done."

I did my best to convince him that not only could Jesus save him, but He longed to reveal His love to him. I urged him to surrender to Christ and receive His love right then, right there, just as Mama had done in that hospital room.

He refused. As far as I know, He never humbled himself and received the grace and salvation of Jesus. Grace doesn't care where you've been or what you've done. Even a monster like this man isn't beyond the ability of God's grace to transform. Everyone is just one prayer of faith away from freedom and a fresh start.

So there's not a more descriptive word for grace than amazing! As John Newton, the former slave trader turned preacher, wrote, *"Amazing grace, how sweet the sound, that saved a wretch like me. I once was lost but now am found, 'twas blind but now I see."*

Grace still amazes me! It was the grace of God that plucked me as a brand out of the fire and gave me a life better than I could have imagined. I hope that everyone who reads my story of God's redemption will experience the same and even more in your life.

I believe every reader will experience a touch from God. But there are some who will identify with my struggle very personally. Perhaps it's you. Are you living in your own personal place of torment? Maybe you can't change your circumstances at the moment, but if you'll serve Jesus, give your entire self to God, He will save you. He will help you and make a way for you. He'll give you His life; new life!

He doesn't love me more than He loves you. If you feel rejected, like no one loves you or values you, God will be your father and your mama. Jesus loves you when no one else loves you. He accepts you if everyone else rejects you. He will deliver you from the torments of hell and teach you to live in the glories of Heaven. And He will save your family, like He saved mine!

Impartation

Let Jesus deliver you from the hurt and the pain. Let Him deliver you from the bitter unforgiveness that fuels despair and anger. Give it to Jesus. Give yourself to Jesus. Right now.

Maybe you can't identify with the torment of my story (I hope you can't), but you still need the life of Jesus. Jesus died for all, including you. He took all of our sin upon Himself and paid the penalty for every act of rebellion and disobedience. He went to hell in your place, so you don't have to go there when you die or continue to live there now. Three days after they crucified Him, He rose again. And now, because He lives, you can live!

He is alive, seated at the right hand of God in Heaven, and praying for you right now. Don't miss it, He is calling you, through my story, to receive His life. Will you receive Jesus? Will you trust your life to Him? I can promise you, you'll never regret it! I've met many people who regretted not following Christ earlier, but never anyone who regretted surrendering to Him too soon.

How about you? Will you pray with me right now as I prayed with Oral Roberts long ago? If you'll believe the Lord Jesus in your heart and confess with your mouth, you'll receive the life of Christ. This is what Romans 10:9 and10 says,

> *"That if thou shalt confess with thy mouth the Lord Jesus, and shalt believe in thine heart that God hath raised him from the dead, thou shalt be saved. For with the heart man believeth unto righteousness; and with the mouth confession is made unto salvation."*

Join me in prayer, right now. Say out loud wherever you are: *"O Lord, be merciful to me. I am a sinner and I need a Savior. I believe, Jesus! I believe in Your coming, Your death, and Your resurrection. Come into my heart and save me from my sins. I repent and receive Christ now as my personal Savior. I declare Jesus is, from this moment, Lord of my life! I will live for Him forever by His grace. Amen."*

If you believe and receive Him right now, He is saving you! A miracle of miracles is happening to you! Lift your hands to God and praise Him!

I pray you will receive now in the mighty name of Jesus! You need to read your Bible and pray every day. Pray for the Lord to put you in a good, Spirit-filled church under the leadership of pastors who will help you become a true disciple of Jesus. As soon as you can,

Camp Tribe!

you need to obey the Lord and get water baptized. Right now ask the Lord to baptize you in the precious Holy Spirit.

I love you, and I've prayed for you. I believe the Lord is going to work through you as He has worked through me. My prayer is that you will be an even stronger witness for Jesus than I've been. I pray you will heal the sick, cast out devils, raise the dead, and win many souls to Christ Jesus!

I am so very proud of the decision you are making and of the way you are seeking to know the Lord. Keep going after Jesus! Let no one or nothing keep you from following Jesus. Pursue Him and you'll never regret it. One day soon I'll get to talk it over with you in Heaven. Perhaps we can share a heavenly Pepsi and Moon Pie together!

CHAPTER FOURTEEN

LEGACY

Larry Nix was more than my dad. He was my best friend. Year's ago we were staying with some friends during a series of meetings. I had stayed there many times before but this was Dad's first time staying in the home. This generous couple's son was around 8 years old and was in and out of the room as we fellowshipped around the table following the evening services.

My friend told us the next morning that when he tucked him into bed that night, his son asked about Dad. He told him, "You know. That's Keith's dad."

His son's reply still makes me smile today, "That can't be his dad! They act too much like friends." I am eternally grateful for the dad the Lord gave to me!

I often say to church audiences, I've slept through more church services than they'll ever attend. Generally speaking it is true. In almost all of those services, my dad was the preacher. Now, don't misunderstand, it wasn't that he was boring. Not at all. The issue was my age. When I was a child, it seems we were in church every night of the week. And those services weren't of the modern hour and half max variety. They lasted for hours. I'm not complaining. I am very thankful.

As an adult, I was with Dad in hundreds of services. Many where he was preaching, others I was preaching, and many others where we were preaching together. We both enjoyed the tag-team preaching times. We never pre-planned those messages. The closest we came was a potential topic or biblical story to work from. To many it seemed we worked from an outline, but our only plan was to follow the leading of the Holy Spirit. People loved it, we loved it, and the Lord always honored those times with a strong anointing.

Some see all the thousands of miles, long services, getting home late and up early for school the next morning as a negative. I view it as a great blessing. How many children get to go to work with their mom and dad every day? I value the time we spent together as a family, the times when it was just him and me traveling together, and the times when he traveled with Margie and me. We traveled to many states and ministered together in many places through the years and had a blast. I miss those days!

While Larry Nix wasn't a perfect man, he was most definitely a great man. Ask his wife and his children! Ask those who knew him best. He had his struggles. We are aware of them. He had to deal with issues throughout his life, most of which were the residue of his childhood. Like the rest of us, he didn't always get it right. But his heart was after God and for his people. He loved his family, and his family loved him.

One thing that inspires me most about Dad is the realization that despite being abandoned by his biological dad and abused by his stepdad, he became a great dad. He broke out of the pattern that he experienced and proved you don't have to repeat your pain. He would tell you, and I am a witness, that it is the grace of God. The power of redemption took a rejected and battered boy and made him a bulwark of strength and safety.

On April 21, 2020, at 7:54 PM, this outstanding fighter laid down his weapons, drew his last breath, and gloriously entered the Heaven he preached so long. Surrounded by family and special friends, the tangible presence of the Lord marked his home-going. It was both a sad and a joyous occasion. Sad, of course, because it was too soon for him to leave. We miss him terribly. Yet, joyous, because he belonged to the Lord and the Lord came for him. He didn't die! He took a journey that we will also take one day. We didn't "lose" him. He lives where we are headed. And, when we arrive, Dad will be part of the welcoming committee!

The day after Dad's passing, the next-door neighbor told my brother-in-law an amazing story.

This was during the Covid shut down, and we parked several vehicles all around my parent's house, and she said, "I know what you all were doing last night! You were having church!"

He explained what happened. She gasped and said,

"That explains it!"

She told him how the night before, between 7:30 and 8:00 PM, she heard a loud noise. When she looked out, she saw her front yard was full of doves! She got her mother's attention, and they marveled at the number of doves, all cooing loudly. It seemed to us then, and still today, that it was a sign from the Lord. I believe it was a physical sign of a glorious, Heavenly escort sent to carry Dad to his eternal reward.

Those last days were emotional, to say the least. As I look back, my heart is gripped by a mixture of sadness, joy, peace, and determination. The latter is increasingly becoming my priority. I am resolved to see Dad's prayers answered. In addition, I am determined to see the prophetic words He gave become our reality! When Dad prophesied you could take it to the bank! I know. I've lived it and I intend to see every prayer and prophecy continue to become reality in my sphere of influence!

Dad didn't want to go to heaven from a hospital, and God answered our prayers by fulfilling his desire. They transported him home on Monday afternoon and just thirty hours later, the angels of the Lord came to transport him to his eternal home. He didn't leave this world quietly. He left rejoicing and giving glory to the Lord.

We prayed, praised, sang, and shared with him testimonies that came in by the hundreds. He could no longer speak, but he expressively acknowledged each testimony. As we read them, he responded with nods and lifting his hands in a wave of praise. Then, he did something that puzzled. He would reach up, toward the top of his head, with his hand, as if grabbing something and then laying it down in front of him. We tried asking him if he needed something. We couldn't figure out why he kept repeating this action. We suggested a few possibilities for him, and he would shake his head in disagreement with every guess. Soon, we stopped asking so it wouldn't frustrate him over his inability to speak. Later, mom realized what it was.

The Early Days

He often spoke of looking forward to the day when he could join with the Elders in laying his crown before the Lord and saying, *"Thou art worthy, O Lord. To receive glory and honour and power..." [Revelation 4:11]*

So, as we read each testimony, Dad showed with what strength remained that all the praise and glory belongs to Jesus. This one action speaks of the essence of his walk with Lord. He was well aware of his own inability, but even more confident in the power of God! The touch of God's anointing on his life was unique and powerful. He knew the voice of God and showed an amazing willingness to obey.

I thought it would be a blessing for you to read a few of the testimonies we read to Dad the afternoon of his home-going:

Heading To Oklahoma For Revival

"Bro. Larry is so dear to my heart. Hearing his testimony every year at Camp (since 1999) has impacted my life tremendously. I know that I have received healing from hearing his story. Getting to know him and Sis. Ramona through the years has been a wonderful part of my life. They've become family. I loved hearing his stories. One of my favorite memories is when I could drive him home from a meeting. He told me story after story of things he had seen and witnessed - miracles and funny stories. He kept me laughing! But, his conversations always went back to Jesus. His love for the Lord was evident. As is his love for his family. I love that if you think of Bro. Larry you automatically think of Sis. Ramona, too! They're a shining example of integrity, faith, and what a family looks like."

Carla C.

"I have loved getting to know Pastor Larry and Pastor Ramona over these years. I've been with them on EDA and while traveling with Pastors Keith and Margie! There is a specific day that really impacted my life. I remember it was shortly after Katelyn and I started getting really plugged into The Lift. I was a new Christian and Pastor Larry came to The Lift. I remember we were all in the altar praying and seeking God - and he gave me a word for my family that day that I still declare as I pray for them. "That I would see my entire family saved" - And over the last 6 years I keep watching it unfold and I always remember back to that service. He actually gave Katelyn the same word in the altar and that may have been the first time we met him - her and I were on opposite sides of the altar (he wouldn't have known Katelyn and I were sisters). He confirmed it through her and since that day I have just watched as God fulfills that word in amazement. I'm so grateful to know him and Pastor Ramona! They've been so precious. Every time I see them they're both so full of genuine love for people and for Jesus. His testimony has impacted me so much, especially in hearing the forgiveness God brought him to with his family - I know in my own life that has brought me healing."

Taylor B.

"It is impossible for me to say all that Brother Larry & Sister Ramona mean to me! They have been my pastors for over 30 years, (and also are my Aunt & uncle). God has taught me so very much about his love & mercy by being a part of their ministry, about believing God's word no matter how things look in the natural & about being faithful to what God has called you to do! If you know Brother Larry, you know how much he loved Brother Hall, so for me Brother Larry is my Brother Hall! I love them both so much & am believing for a complete miracle!"

Kendall H.

"From a young child I remember, Bro. Larry's anointing. He would preach at dad's church and always bring a timely word and help (not to mention a good dose of humor like only he can dish out). He has prophesied many times to me and my family and it's come to pass. He's been a true friend to my family, an elder in the faith, and a prophet."

Dean L.

"The first year that Pastor Josh & I attended youth camp & brought Family Worship Center youth with us (2 years ago)... I still remember the conversation in the van on the way home... all

these teenagers talked about was Pastor Larry & his testimony...& how they wished he could come preach at our church. I was just amazed at how these young teenagers enjoyed hearing the oldest speaker so much... just goes to show you it's all about the anointing. Then when we came last year... the youth that had been before kept talking about how awesome your dad was & how they couldn't wait till the night Pastor Larry spoke. Pastor Larry is a special & anointed man..."

Corinna C.

"I hope I am half the man Bro. Larry is! There are so many things I learned from him and so many things I aspire to be because of him. Most of all, I want to have the kind of relationship with Jesus that Pastor Larry has. They are true best friends!"

Zach C.

"One of the best memories I have is going to Sam's Club with Pastor Larry and Pastor Ramona to get food for youth camp. They had me laughing the whole time. When he preaches he has this way of making you laugh one second and cry the next. Every time he shares his testimony, it opens your eyes to God's love and the beautiful thoughtfulness He puts into His plan for our lives. It's

hard for me to get my head around how he can be so fierce and yet so humble and meek. He is truly a wonderful man of God. Pastor Larry and Pastor Ramona have a very special place in all of our hearts."

Samuel F.

"Pastor Larry has had a huge impact on my life and on the lives of all my family. He has spoken many powerful prophetic words to me that have come to pass, and are coming to pass. We love him and the Nix family very much. He is a true prophet and general in the Faith!"

Christian W.

"Pastor Larry is a man of honor. A man of integrity. A man of God! One of the greatest preachers I know! And the best pastor ever! Bro. Larry and Sis. Ramona, and all the Nix's, are like family! My spiritual mom and dad! Bro. Larry has always been faithful to his calling...and always will! I have been so blessed to be part of their lives since 1985. They took me under their wings when I was so young in the Lord! They've prayed for me and with me through the good times and the bad...To see the Lord through Bro. Larry's eyes, his great anointing, no words could express! Mark had the greatest respect and admiration for

Bro. Larry. As do I! Mark often talked of their travels together. Their laughter. Their tears. The things they saw and experienced. He truly missed you both and spending time with you. The stories Bro. Larry would tell of his ministry. How God moved repeatedly in his life! The visions! The healings! The man you see inside the four walls, is the same you see outside the four walls. There is no disguise in his faith and beliefs!"

Nancy M.

"I have always seen Bro. Larry as a mighty man of God. There have been many meetings, camp meetings and youth camp services when he spoke the Word of the Lord boldly and powerfully, bringing everyone into a heavy glory of God's presence.

He has spoken and prophesied over me numerous times, encouraging me in the Lord. One time, in particular, he said, "This year is going to be one of the greatest years of your life. The Lord is doing many things, and he will do a great thing for you in August of this year. It will change your life and affect your ministry like never before."

That year, August came and passed, with me wondering what became of the word he had spoken. It wasn't until October that I discovered the power behind this word. I received a call from my mother. "Luke, I have something to tell you," she said in a very unsure voice. "I have been waiting since August to tell you, and I just can't hold back anymore. I asked the Lord to save me, and to forgive me, and to come into my life."

I immediately thanked God with tears! "Momma! This is the best news I have ever heard! I am so thankful, and happy! I love you so much!" I cried. I had been praying for her to be saved as far back as I can remember. I begged and pleaded for her to come to church as just a little child. Every time I saw a shooting star, my wish was for her to be born again and have a relationship with Jesus Christ! This was not what I was expecting when I received this word, but I am so happy Bro. Larry was used as God's voice to give this message to me, reassuring me He had not forgotten about me. It changed my life! God really hears the prayers of His people, and He answers them! Even after 30-plus years of praying, God never forgets! He always has a plan!

Thank you, Bro. Larry, for being such a man after God's own heart! You allowed Him to use you to bless me so much! I love you, sir, and wish you well! May the healing virtue of Almighty God flow through your body and strengthen you, in Jesus' name!"

Luke G.

"Brother Larry has always been an inspiration. One thing among many that stands out in my memory some years ago I had a bout with bursitis. The only way I could sleep was sitting upright, leaning forward on a pillow the doctor gave me a cortisone shot and told me not to call back it was going to get worse before it got better. Brother Larry was preaching at our church that night he prayed for me and not only did it not get worse, I had no more pain, and these many years later I've had no more pain."

Linda L.

"When we would go to camp meeting at Bro. Hall's.... Bro. & Sis. Nix was always there and they are such a blessing!! Always loved to hear Bro. Nix preach! the anointing was always so thick, and so many blessed. Sis. Nix is always a joy to hear minister, she's such a beautiful soul. They are such a wonderful blessing to so many, and oh what an example!! these are memories that will be cherished a lifetime! We want to say...Thank you for inspiring and touching our life in ways you know not of, I'm sure that applies to so many lives. You have paved the way of divine excellence, and guidance that we can embrace every moment, that will forever be chiseled in our life! God certainly elected you both as... God's

Generals! With very much honor and love we're proud to say you have fed into our life and forever it will remain."

Mitch and Sandra C.

"His testimony is major for me. No matter how many times I have heard it, it is proof of God's providential care, God's desire to fulfill His purposes in our lives and God's great love for us."

Lynette E.

"He was doing a service at Fall Creek Full Gospel church in Jonesville, North Carolina. I was fairly new to the "Pentecostal way"... lol... I had been suffering with lots of acid reflux because of the flap in the top of my stomach not closing properly. I was going to church that night and I had ran out of the meds that I had been taking for that. So I thought I will just stop at this little convenience store and get a pack of Rolaids to help me get thru the night. I threw them in my purse and proceeded to church. During that service, Brother Larry, said to me, "Little sister come here." I came to the front of the church and he said while doing a circular motion with his finger, "there's something going on right here in your stomach but the Lord is healing you right

now!" I felt heat go down my throat into the top of my stomach and come back out. I never suffered with acid reflux again!

Several months later, while cleaning out my purse, I found that packet of unopened Rolaids. The foil was worn off of each end of the roll where it had been rolling around in my purse. I remember thinking about the reason I stopped to get them and was still amazed and very thankful to have never had a reason to open them. To this day, 20+ years, I have not eaten another Rolaid or taken any reflux medications! God is so good! I am thankful for Larry's service and obedience to the Lord!"

Gail N.

Glory to God! These are just a handful of the hundreds of testimonies that came in via social media the last couple of days of Dad's life. Perhaps you have a testimony. I would love to hear how the Lord touched you through Dad's obedience.

Let me share with you one more testimony of the Lord working through Dad. In one revival meeting, a blind lady came and her husband requested Dad pray for her. As he prayed, he declared what the Lord said to him. In the hearing of all in attendance, he told the woman that the Lord said she would receive her sight that night! He prayed, yet nothing changed. Even though she was still blind, he simply moved on - knowing he had obeyed. He was a bit troubled by it and asked the Lord about it on the drive home. He didn't receive an answer, so he just resolved that since he obeyed, it was in the Lord's hands. The next morning, he received a phone call from the local pastor telling him what happened.

The pastor told dad he had just gotten in to bed a bit after midnight, when there was loud knocking on his front door. Going to the door, he saw the blind lady and her husband.

As he opened the door, the lady grabbed his arm, pulling him outside. She said, "Pastor! Come look at the stars with me!" They stood on the porch for almost an hour, looking, laughing, and rejoicing in the goodness of the Lord.

Healed! He asked her how it manifested. She told him that as she was preparing for bed, she chose to praise God for her healing, even though it hadn't manifested yet. Suddenly her sight was restored and she could see! Hallelujah! Dad rejoiced with the pastor and praised God for His faithfulness! I love Dad's bold obedience. He inspires me to be just as bold in trusting the Lord's voice.

His legacy lives on in the lasting impact of his obedience to God. He also lives on through his biological children, grandchildren and great grandchildren. And his legacy lives on through thousands across the globe who became spiritual children and carry a touch of the glory of God released in them by Dad's "Yes" to Jesus.

He adopted Paul's words in Acts 26:19 as his own personal mantra, *"...I was not disobedient unto the heavenly vision."* My prayer is we will say these words with great confidence throughout our journey, and all the way to the end.

My prayer for you is to receive healing and complete freedom from everything that torments you. Dad told his story, regardless of personal cost, for your healing. He shared his personal pain hoping his story will help you discover and walk in the freedom that only comes from Christ Jesus.

Keith, Mona, Monika, and Stephen Nix

My hope is not only that you receive personal freedom but that you also partner with God to help free others from the torments of hell and bring them to the glories of Heaven. It will thrill Dad to greet you in Heaven and talk it over with you! It will thrill all of his family also! Let's make it a date! Of course, we can't set the day on our calendars, but we can commit ourselves completely to Christ and meet together around His throne when He determines it is time!

I'm looking forward to enjoying the glories of Heaven with Dad and you! In the meantime, I would love to hear how Dad's story has touched your life!

Family At 50th Wedding Anniversary

60 YEARS OF PREACHING JESUS!

Cocke County, TN Courthouse • Circa 1968

ABOUT THE AUTHOR

KEITH NIX is a husband, dad, pastor, evangelist, and author whose passion is to reach, teach, and elevate others into their full God-given potential. He and his wife Margie live in Sevierville, Tennessee with their daughter, Isabella where they planted The Lift Church in 2013. Keith and Margie Nix have also led a summer youth camp for over twenty five years. Camp Tribe has impacted thousands of students from all over the world, calling them to live a lifestyle of revival. In addition they have traveled the globe ministering at crusades and various missions outreaches. They have also hosted a summer internship over the past two decades, pouring into young leaders. To learn more about Keith Nix visit his website at *keithnix.org*

WEBSITE
KEITHNIX.ORG | SOCIAL MEDIA
@KEITHNIXTV

THE LIFT MEDIA

STAY UP-TO-DATE WITH THE LATEST FROM PASTORS KEITH & MARGIE NIX!

WEBSITE: THELIFTCHURCH.TV
YOTUBE: YOUTUBE.COM/THELIFT

ALSO FIND THE LIFT CHURCH ON ROKU AND VISIT YOUR APP STORE TO DOWNLOAD THE FREE LIFT CHURCH APP!

Printed in Great Britain
by Amazon